The Stations of the
Resurrection

RONALD C. GIBBINS

The Stations of the Resurrection

Devotions for use at Easter

Drawings by
DAVID M. CAINK

THE LITURGICAL PRESS
Collegeville, Minnesota

Cover icon: Andrei Rublev, The Savior.
Cover design by Joshua J. Jeide, O.S.B.

Selection of the hymn texts on pages 19, 37, 45, 55, 65, 76, and 86 by David Klingeman, O.S.B.

Copyright © Ronald C. Gibbins, 1988. First published in Great Britain jointly by Foundery Press, Peterborough, and St. Paul Publications, Slough. This edition for the United States and Canada published by The Liturgical Press, Collegeville, Minnesota.

Printed in the United States of America.

Library of Congress Cataloging-in-Publication Data
Gibbons, Ronald C.
   The Stations of the Resurrection : devotions for use at Easter /
Ronald C. Gibbons ; drawings by David M. Caink.
      p. cm.
   ISBN 0-8146-1775-1
   1. Jesus Christ—Appearances—Prayer-books and devotions— English.
2. Easter—Prayer-books and devotions—English.   I. Title.
BT490.G5   1989   88-27111
232.9′7—dc19   CIP

Contents

Preface

IT was while I was on retreat at the Cistercian Monastery of Saint Bernard, Leicestershire, that I wrote the first draft of *The Stations of the Resurrection*. The Stations are designed to draw Christians together ecumenically so that our spirituality may become one and aid our growing together. I am indebted to the Rev. David M. Caink of Kings Lynn for his line drawings which illustrate the Stations with such imagination; also to Mr Edward Fittall for advice and editing, and to Mrs Nona Spackman and Miss Maria Stack for help in typing the manuscript. The Scripture Passages for Study are from *The New English Bible*, Second Edition 1970, and printed here by permission of Oxford and Cambridge University Presses.

I hope that these devotions will assist the formation of faith in the Risen Christ in all who use them, and that they will enrich the forty days from Easter to Ascension to great spiritual profit.

> Ronald C. Gibbins
> *Minister*
> *Wesley's Chapel, London*

Introduction

SINCE the fifteenth century the Catholic tradition, the Franciscan especially, has used the devotional method known as at the Stations of the Cross. It is a method which gives to faithful people the opportunity to follow Jesus in the agonising experiences which led him to Calvary and crucifixion. The Stations focus on incidents in the Passion narrative and normally take the form of representational images at fixed positions on the walls of churches. There may be variations in number – for example, at Birnau on Lake Constance in Switzerland, where the Stations are in the rococo style of c. 1724, there are only eight – but usually there are fourteen (as quantified by Pope Clement XII) representing nine events in Scripture and five from tradition.

This model for devotion, useful to the faithful for so long, need not be confined to that one part of God's redeeming work; it can be extended by similar method to the celebration of our Lord's Resurrection. Here, then, the Stations that follow are for the period of the traditional forty days from Easter Sunday to the day of Ascension.

The appearances of the risen Christ may be classified conveniently under seven headings if, to fulfil our purpose and for reasons developed later, we include also the experience of Paul on the Damascus road even though some two years separate it from the forty days.

The Stations together form a seven-fold pattern of celebration which extends through the six Sundays of the forty days to a culmination at the Ascension. The shape of a Station is as follows:

(1) the reading of the Scripture text;

Introduction

(2) a brief homily to expand the meaning and prepare our
    devotional thought;
(3) a prayer and, after a silence, the basis for meditation;
(4) the suggestion of a fitting hymn.

The book has various possibilities of use. It can be used for
private devotion, by a house group, or by a congregation in
church, and since (varying interpretations apart) there is
nothing theologically controversial in the Resurrection as an
article of faith, it can be used ecumenically as the encourager of
Christians of different traditions to share their churches and
worship together in one faith of the risen Christ. Although
visual aids are not a necessary part, some groups or congregations might find them helpful and consider putting up pictorial
Stations – an empty cross, say, with a simple drawing – in
different parts of the room or church. Others, wishing to devise
an imaginative and extended programme, might look upon
music, drama, or even liturgical dance as a fitting supplement.

Whether the book is read straight through, as might be done
in private, or used as a weekly sequence, as might be the proba-
bility for groups or congregations, may it be a means of our Lord
himself blessing us as we ponder his resurrection appearances.
May we be made ready to receive him into our hearts when he
makes himself known to us. May a deepened faith send us out,
as his first disciples were sent, with true light into a dark and
sinful world.

1. The Empty Tomb

The central character of this Station is
MARY OF MAGDALA

Scripture passage for study
John 20: 1–18

Passages for further study
Matthew 28: 1–15
Mark 16: 1–13
Luke 24: 1–11

Scripture passage for study
JOHN 20: 1–18

EARLY on the Sunday morning, while it was still dark, Mary of Magdala came to the tomb. She saw that the stone had been moved away from the entrance, and ran to Simon Peter and the other disciple, the one whom Jesus loved. 'They have taken the Lord out of his tomb,' she cried, 'and we do not know where they have laid him.' So Peter and the other set out and made their way to the tomb. They were running side by side, but the other disciple outran Peter and reached the tomb first. He peered in and saw the linen wrappings lying there, but did not enter. Then Simon Peter came up, following him, and he went into the tomb. He saw the linen wrappings lying, and the napkin which had been over his head, not lying with the wrappings but rolled together in a place by itself. Then the disciple who had reached the tomb first went in too, and he saw and believed; until then they had not understood the scriptures, which showed that he must rise from the dead.

So the disciples went home again; but Mary stood at the tomb outside, weeping. As she wept, she peered into the tomb; and she saw two angels in white sitting there, one at the head, and one at the feet, where the body of Jesus had lain. They said to her, 'Why are you weeping?' She answered, 'They have taken my Lord away, and I do not know where they have laid him.' With these words she turned round and saw Jesus standing there, but did not recognize him. Jesus said to her, 'Why are you weeping? Who is it you are looking for?' Thinking it was the gardener, she said, 'If it is you, sir, who removed him, tell me where you have laid him, and I will take him away.' Jesus said, 'Mary!' She turned to him and said, 'Rabbuni!' (which is Hebrew for 'My Master'). Jesus said, 'Do not cling to me, for I have not yet ascended to the Father. But go to my brothers, and tell them that I am now ascending to my Father and your Father, my God and your God.' Mary of Magdala went to the disciples with her news: 'I have seen the Lord!' she said, and gave them his message.

Homily

JOHN 20: 18 *Mary of Magdala went to the disciples with her news: 'I have seen the Lord!' she said, and gave them his message.*

THE world today may see us either as the happiest of enlightened and assured Christian believers or the saddest and most deluded of pathetic fools. The very act of reading this book means that we are taking certain steps. They are all-important steps; we are running to the tomb of Jesus to see if it is occupied or empty. In doing that, we identify ourselves with Mary of Magdala, with Peter, and with John the beloved disciple.

Mary has been to the tomb early. She runs back distraught to Peter and John. 'They have taken the Lord ...!' There is immediate response. Peter and John race towards the tomb. Mary is behind. John is faster than Peter, perhaps because Peter – who has been called the Big Fisherman – is heavier in build. John is the first to arrive, but he merely peers in and sees the linen wrappings; it is the bold Peter who is the first to enter and to observe, not only the way the wrappings are placed, but how the head napkin has been rolled up and set aside.

That, then, is the sequence of events so far. We read that John was the first both to see *and* believe, but we must bear in mind that this is a statement made with hindsight. For our present purpose we focus on Mary, our central character, but for whom that race to the tomb might not have happened. When the others go home, she stays behind. It is her experience that stands so majestically for the witness of the resurrection.

In the garden of the tomb she sees someone whom she supposes is the gardener. 'Who are you looking for?' – the very question to be expected from the gardener of a cemetery. 'If it is you, sir, who removed him, tell me where you have laid him, and I will take him away.' One word, the utterance of her name, is enough to bring her instant recognition of her risen Lord. In her response, 'My Master', she not only declares her recognition of Jesus; she confirms her allegiance. She is told what to do. In her doing it, we have our text: 'Mary of Magdala went to the disciples with her news: "I have seen the Lord!" she said, and gave them his message.'

This premier Resurrection appearance has a special quality. It is of the rarest beauty and, in its simplicity, for ever fresh. It has never ceased to thrill the hearts and hold the minds of generation after generation of Christian believers. At first, Mary had not known him. She had been looking for a missing body in the form she had previously known, that could be seen and touched and clung to humanly. His presence, when it was revealed to her, was in a different way; it was a dawning of absolute light out of absolute darkness, a presence relating in a new, a heightened, an intensified way, a presence that could be taken into her deepest self to become irremovably a part of her own being. A lesson for us is that Jesus will make himself known in ways of his choosing. In whatever way he comes, and however unexpected the encounter, we are to be ready and open to receive him.

What matters most in any witness to the Resurrection is the end result. Every celebration of Easter sends us an open invitation to experience anew the light of the risen Christ. That light is the same light that confirmed the faith of the first disciples and sent them out active into the world. It is the dismissive light, from which all shadows in ourselves will flee; it is the refining light, in which our spiritual perceptions will grow; it is the inextinguishable light, the light that we, as present-day disciples, are called to carry into a thousand and one dark tombs that disfigure God's world even if we often recoil from the suffering and sadness we find in such disfigurement.

Where does the darkness of the tomb exist? Where have we buried Jesus? Wherever a blindness to the will of God has led us: to a tolerance of poverty, to the waste of God's gifts, to greed, to violence, to the misuse of power, to cruelty, to mindless bigotry, to the heart's perversion in ways without number; those, and many another, are the tombs that will for ever be dark till the light is brought. It is there, in all the conditions that deaden human life, that we must bear witness to the light of the Jesus who is risen, is alive, and is the overcomer of every darkness. It is there that we must stand with the enlightenment of Mary, saying in the voice of allegiance, 'My Master', and in our lives show the evidence of his Peace, his Love, and his Salvation.

Devotions

Prayer
Lord Jesus,
   the conqueror of death,
   who came living from the tomb to be our Saviour Christ:
   speak to us when, like Mary of Magdala,
   we stand thinking ourselves alone
   in life's dark wilderness.
   Speak to us by name, as you spoke to Mary,
   that we may recognise as she did
   your living presence;
   and sharing her joy, copying her allegiance,
   may go with her enlightenment into the world,
   saying 'I have seen the Lord!' *Amen*

Silence

Meditation

Let us try to picture the biblical scene, to see and to feel
the utter desolation of the first disciples after the death of
Jesus.
Let us think of circumstances in our own lives which bring
darkness of the spirit, which attack our belief, which let
cynicism take hold of us, which lead to despair.
Let us think of circumstances in the wider world, read about
in newspapers or seen on the television screen, which fill us
with a sad frustration or a helpless anger.
Let us think of Mary at the tomb of Jesus.

Let us think of her forlorn bewilderment when she finds that the body of Jesus is there no longer.
Let us see Mary grieving in the garden.
Let us hear the voice of Jesus calling Mary by name.
Let us see despair changed suddenly to joy, as she recognises her own name.
Let us rejoice in our risen Saviour, whose vital light in and through us and all his people will cast out every darkness to the ends of the earth . . .
Let us say in our hearts: 'My Master'.

Hymn

1   Christ the Lord is risen today;
Christians, haste your vows to pay;
Offer now your praises meet
At the Paschal Victim's feet;
For the sheep the Lamb has bled,
Sinless in the sinner's stead.
Christ the Lord is risen on high;
Now he lives, no more to die.

2   Christ the victim undefiled,
God and sinners reconciled;
When in strange and awful strife
Met together death and life;
Christians, on this happy day
Haste with joy your vows to pay.
Christ the Lord is risen on high;
Now he lives, no more to die.

3   Come, rejoicing Mary, say
What you saw along the way.
"I beheld, where Christ had lain,
Empty tomb and angels twain;
I beheld the glory bright
Of the rising Lord of light:

The Empty Tomb

> Christ the Lord is risen on high;
> Now he lives, no more to die."

4 Christ, who once for sinners bled,
Now the first-born from the dead,
Throned in endless might and power,
Lives and reigns for evermore.
Hail, eternal hope on high!
Hail, our King of victory!
Hail, our Prince of life adored!
Help and save us, gracious Lord!

Victimae Paschali Laudes, attr. to Wipo of Burgundy (10th century), tr. Jane Elizabeth Leeson, 1809–1881, alt.

Suggested hymn tune: *VICTIMAE PASCHALI*

2. The Emmaus Walk

The central character of this Station is
CLEOPAS

====================================

Scripture passage for study
Luke 24: 13–35

Passage for further study
Mark 16: 12–13

Scripture passage for study

LUKE 24: 13–35

THAT same day two of them were on their way to a village called Emmaus, which lay about seven miles from Jerusalem, and they were talking about all these happenings. As they talked and discussed it with one another, Jesus himself came up and walked along with them; but something held their eyes from seeing who it was. He asked them, 'What is it you are debating as you walk?' They halted, their faces full of gloom, and one, called Cleopas, answered, 'Are you the only person staying in Jersualem not to know what has happened there in the last few days?' 'What do you mean?' he said. 'All this about Jesus of Nazareth,' they replied, 'a prophet powerful in speech and action before God and the whole people; how our chief priests and rulers handed him over to be sentenced to death, and crucified him. But we had been hoping that he was the man to liberate Israel. What is more, this is the third day since it happened, and now some women of our company have astounded us: they went early to the tomb, but failed to find his body, and returned with a story that they had seen a vision of angels who told them he was alive. So some of our people went to the tomb and found things just as the women had said; but him they did not see.'

'How dull are you!' he answered. 'How slow to believe all that the prophets said! Was the Messiah not bound to suffer thus before entering upon his glory?' Then he began with Moses and all the prophets, and explained to them the passages which referred to himself in every part of the scriptures.

By this time they had reached the village to which they were going, and he made as if to continue his journey, but they pressed him: 'Stay with us, for evening draws on, and the day is almost over.' So he went in to stay with them. And when he had sat down with them at the table, he took bread and said the blessing; he broke the bread, and offered it to them. Then their eyes were opened, and they recognized him; and he vanished from their sight. They said to one another, 'Did we not feel our hearts on fire as he talked with us on the road and explained the scriptures to us?'

Without a moment's delay they set out and returned to Jerusalem. There they found that the Eleven and the rest of the company had assembled, and were saying, 'It is true: the Lord has risen; he has appeared to Simon.' Then they gave their account of the events of their journey and told how he had been recognized by them at the breaking of the bread.

Homily

LUKE 24: 32 *Did we not feel our hearts on fire as he talked with us on the road and explained the scriptures to us?*

FOR the second Station of the Resurrection we move from the garden tomb to the open road that leads to a village. The name of the village is one of the best-known in Christendom: Emmaus, lying some seven miles from Jerusalem.

Two disciples, who have not been previously mentioned in the Gospel narrative, are walking from Jerusalem to Emmaus in the evening of the third day after the crucifixion of Jesus. Like others, they had held great expectations of Jesus, even thinking that he would bring about the liberation of Israel. They are joined by a stranger. It is beyond them to understand how anyone coming from Jerusalem at such a time could be in ignorance of the appalling events that had happened there so recently. The stranger actually asks them what they mean. They give him a despondent explanation of what has happened so far; how it is now the evening of the third day; how the women early at the tomb have told their astonishing tale of the tomb empty; how others also have been to the tomb but seen nothing of Jesus either dead or alive. Even when this stranger begins all at once to expound the scriptures, and in doing so all but declares his identity, they remain uncomprehending. Yet, at the same time, a strange and inexplicable feeling comes to them. Dull, slow in the uptake they may be, but so impressed are they by the manner of the stranger, and by what he says, that later they declare in Jerusalem: 'Did we not feel our hearts on fire as he talked with us on the road and explained the scriptures to us?' (so giving us our key text). No doubt in their kindled state of mind they are eager to hear more. Jesus indicates his intention to continue his journey (he is always moving ahead, always leading; there is a mission to fulfil), but they persuade him to come in and stay with them. And there, at the family table, as Jesus blesses the bread of the evening meal in a way they have heard before, and breaks it in a way they have seen before, a full recognition dawns on them at last; it is Jesus himself, and he had been beside them on the road all the while! 'Did we not feel our hearts on fire as he talked with us on the road . . .?'

Here, then, is the second resurrection appearance. The two of them had probably been witnesses of the worst that had happened outside Jerusalem. At that time, they would surely have felt that God had abandoned Jesus and his followers, that evil had triumphed over good, and that love had fallen a victim to the forces of hatred. God's answer had come. Having experienced so deeply-felt a letdown in Jerusalem, Cleopas and his companion had been given a heart-kindling uplift where, even if the hope had been in them, they might least have expected it to come, on their own well-known homeward road.

Already, Jesus had appeared to Mary of Magdala in the garden and called her by name; now, as though he were any ordinary traveller, he had joined company and walked along the highway. He had conversed as an engaging stranger, and in due time, as an invited guest at the supper table, he had made himself known in the familiar way of his blessing and breaking the bread. This way of opening their eyes to see him and their hearts to receive him, having its link to the Jewish community meal they had shared with him as his followers, is in its mature development the same blessing and breaking of bread by which we too know Jesus our host in his resurrection presence at the Eucharist which is for all believers. By means of it we too walk the Emmaus road and know our hearts on fire as he talks to us.

This Station of the Resurrection gives us all a special responsibility to continue the apostolic mission. Our personal highways can be like the Emmaus road; where others walk with us who have not yet seen the Lord, ours is the privilege to reveal him. The witness of Cleopas on his return to Jerusalem was vital to others. Our witness is as vital on any road where walking it is personal challenge. Roads lead everywhere; to sick-beds, to places of poverty, to where suffering is known. . . . Wherever the roads go, the disciples go, and Christ goes with them. Many are the travellers who have walked their different roads in the Emmaus faith: St Augustine of Hippo, St Francis of Assisi, Martin Luther of Wittenberg, John Wesley of London, and a host also of other witnesses who would all have declared that they saw the Lord and that he walked and talked with them on the way. Emmaus road has a powerful message for us all. It is our pilgrimage road. Having met there our risen Lord, when 'Were not our hearts on fire . . !' we are free to share our resurrection faith with the world.

Devotions

Prayer
Living Lord
    who walking the road to Emmaus
    and talking to two disciples
    set their hearts on fire within them;
    who blessed the bread and broke it
    and uncovered their eyes:
be with us, we pray –
    the risen presence when, by the Eucharist,
    the bread and wine at your table,
    we remember in our grateful hearts
    the body and blood of
    your sacrifice for our sakes.

Be with us, we pray –
    your risen presence guiding us
    through all life's twists and turns;
    the lightener of our load;
    the cleanser of our vision;
    our upholder when we stumble.
As we plead with you to stay,
    help us to know that we can never
    imprison you in our transitory
    cultures and traditions,
    and that only as our hearts are open
    to your measureless, marvellous love
    are we truly your witnessing people,
    your light in the darkness of our time.
    Keep us faithful in service, Lord,
    trustful and eager servants of you our Master,

who alone are the way,
the truth, and the life
for ever. *Amen*

Silence

Meditation

Let us remember
  – that our Lord Jesus, having died for us, came alive also for
    our sake;
  – that there is no road we travel, but the living Christ is there
    beside us;
  – that there is no place we come to, but the living Christ is
    there ahead.
Let us remember with joyful thanks
  – that our Lord Jesus, being once dead, is alive for all time
    and for all people;
  – that as he is with us in all our certainties, so also he stays
    with us even when our doubtings would have him shut out;
  – that, being alive within us,
    he is our peace,
    he is our joy,
    he is the assurance
    that nothing in life
    and nothing in death
    can ever end us
    who share his victory.

Hymn

1 Christ is alive! Let Christians sing.
   His cross stands empty to the sky.
   Let streets and homes with praises ring.
   His love in death shall never die.

The Emmaus Walk

2 Christ is alive! No longer bound
   To distant years in Palestine,
   He comes to claim the here and now
   And conquer every place and time.

3 Not throned above, remotely high
   Untouched, unmoved by human pains,
   But daily, in the midst of life,
   Our Savior with the Father reigns.

4 In every insult, rift, and war
   Where color, scorn or wealth divide,
   He suffers still, yet loves the more
   And lives, though ever crucified.

5 Christ is alive! His Spirit burns
   Through this and every future age,
   Till all creation lives and learns
   His joy, his justice, love and praise.

Brian A. Wren, b. 1936

Suggested hymn tune: *TRURO*

3. The Upper Room

The central characters of this Station are
THE ELEVEN DISCIPLES

Scripture passage for study
John 20: 19–23

Passage for further study
Acts 1: 12–14

Scripture passage for study
JOHN 20: 19–23

LATE that Sunday evening, when the disciples were together behind locked doors, for the fear of the Jews, Jesus came and stood among them. 'Peace be with you!' he said, and then showed them his hands and his side. So when the disciples saw the Lord, they were filled with joy. Jesus repeated, 'Peace be with you!', and said, 'As the Father sent me, so I send you.' Then he breathed on them, saying, 'Receive the Holy Spirit! If you forgive any man's sins, they stand forgiven; if you pronounce them unforgiven, unforgiven they remain.'

Homily

JOHN 20: 19 *Late that Sunday evening, when the disciples were together behind locked doors . . . Jesus came and stood among them.*

THE room we now refer to, known throughout Christendom as the Upper Room, was probably much the same as many another of the upstairs chambers, spacious and well-furnished, that Jewish householders commonly kept for the use of guests and especially guests for the Passover meal. Jesus already knew the availability of the room made ready by a disciple, follower, or well-wisher. When the disciples asked him where they were to get the Passover meal ready, he gave them immediate and straightforward instructions. 'As you go into the city, a man carrying a jar of water will meet you. Follow him into the house he enters, and say to the owner of the house: "The Teacher says to you, Where is the room where my disciples and I will eat the Passover meal?" He will show you a large furnished room upstairs, where you will get everything ready' (Luke 21: 10–12, *GNB*).

Was it back to this same room the disciples came after the crucifixion? Where else, in their fear, could they have gone to be together behind locked doors? This was the room in which Jesus had told them: 'I have wanted so much to eat this Passover meal with you before I suffer. . . .' This was where he had shown them the way to remember him in blessing the bread, breaking it, and pouring the wine. Here they had had their foolish argument and quarrels about who should be thought the greatest among them; from this room his betrayer had departed. . . .

Only if we ourselves have at some time known the reality of deep despair, yet out of it have gained a new and strengthening

34

vision, can we even begin to appreciate the feelings of the disciples when Jesus was suddenly there standing among them in the fast-locked room. 'Peace be with you,' said Jesus. What a significant greeting to men shut in by fear!

From 16: 9 of his gospel, Mark itemises the first three resurrection appearances; first to Mary of Magdala (v9), then to the two on the road to Emmaus (v12), and thirdly to the eleven disciples in the Upper Room. John does not give a precise number present; he points out, and is alone to do so, that Thomas was not present on this occasion and that Jesus came into the room a second time a week later for Thomas to see him, to know him, and to believe (a theme we shall take up at our next Station). Luke's account adds yet more interest. To the eleven disciples he adds an unspecified number referred to as 'the rest of the company' (24: 33). Who they were exactly is not something we can know. That Mary the mother of Jesus was one of the company present at that time can be only tender conjecture. What we know is that Acts 1: 13 does indeed place her by name among the company of believers in the upstairs room only some forty days later, thus putting her within that small Jerusalem Community.

Was Judas present also? He might have been, and if so it may have been then that the realisation of what he had done to Jesus made him take his own life – an unusual step for a religious Jew.

What makes the Upper Room itself as significant to us now as it was then to that first community of witnesses to the resurrection is that it is the elementary model of every Christian sanctuary and every Christian gathering ever since. Our every communion table stands in place of that first table in the Upper Room. Our every Eucharist puts us at one with the first disciples who learnt of the Lord in the Upper Room how they should keep his memory. When we eat the bread and drink the wine of the body and the blood of his sacrifice, we celebrate his life, we give thanks for his death for our sakes – but more, we become ourselves witnesses to the glory of the resurrection, and by receiving him into ourselves are made a vital part of his continuing life of peace and love loosed into a wanting world.

Devotions

Prayer
Lord Jesus,
  who was dead, but overcame death
  and was a living presence to your disciples
  in the first Upper Room:
  open our hearts to the reality
  of your living presence in
  our own Upper Room,
  that setting all fears aside
  we may like those same disciples
  come fully alive in peace and joy.
  Keep us steady in the faith
  and bold for your sake,
  that going as your confident witnesses
  into a hardened world
  we may show that no shut door of the human heart
  is stronger than your love to unlock it,
  and that no earthly power
  can ever stand against the eternal power
  of your resurrection. *Amen*

Silence

Meditation

Let us remember the first Upper Room disciples as recorded in
Acts 1: 13

36

The Upper Room Community

Simon Peter, leader of the Apostles, believed martyred at Rome *c.* AD64, remembered 29th June with Paul.

John, sometimes called 'the Divine', 'the Evangelist' and 'a fisherman', died at Ephesus *c.* AD100, remembered 27th December.

James, John's brother, also a fisherman, died at Jerusalem *c.* AD44, remembered 25th July.

James the less, son of Alphaeus, died at Jerusalem *c.* AD62, remembered 1st May.

Andrew, the first-called disciple, a fisherman, remembered 30th November.

Philip of Bethsaida, remembered 1st May

Thomas the Twin, remembered 21st December.

Bartholomew, who could also be Nathanael 'The Israelite indeed', remembered 24th August.

Matthew, the tax collector, remembered 21st September.

Simon Zealot, the Canaanite, remembered 28th October.

Judas or Jude (not Iscariot), remembered 28th October.

Mary, the Mother of Jesus

Some **other** women disciples

Some family, **brothers** of Jesus.

Hymn

1 That Easter day with joy was bright,
The sun shone out with fairer light,
When to their longing eyes restored,
The apostles saw their risen Lord.

2 His risen flesh with radiance glowed;
His wounded hands and feet he showed;
Those scars their solemn witness gave
That Christ was risen from the grave.

3   O Jesus, King of gentleness,
    Who with your grace our hearts possess
    That we may give you all our days
    The willing tribute of our praise.

4   O Lord of all, with us abide
    In this our joyful Eastertide;
    From every weapon death can wield
    Your own redeemed for ever shield.

5   All praise, to you, O risen Lord,
    Now both by heaven and earth adored;
    To God the Father equal praise,
    And Spirit blest, our songs we raise.

Claro paschali gaudio, Latin (5th century), tr. John Mason Neale, 1818–1866, alt.

Suggested hymn tune: *PUER NOBIS*

4. The Doubting Disciple

The central character of this Station is
THOMAS

Scripture passage for study
John 20: 24–29

Passage for further study
Luke 24: 36–43

Scripture passage for study
JOHN 20: 24–29

ONE of the Twelve, Thomas, that is 'the Twin', was not with the rest when Jesus came. So the disciples told him, 'We have seen the Lord.' He said, 'Unless I see the mark of the nails on his hands, unless I put my finger into the place where the nails were, and my hand into his side, I will not believe it.'

A week later his disciples were again in the room, and Thomas was with them. Although the doors were locked, Jesus came and stood among them, saying, 'Peace be with you!' Then he said to Thomas, 'Reach your finger here; see my hands. Reach your hand here and put it into my side. Be unbelieving no longer, but believe.' Thomas said, 'My Lord and my God!' Jesus said, 'Because you have seen me you have found faith. Happy are they who never saw me and yet have found faith.'

Homily

JOHN 20:29 *Because you have seen me you have found faith.*
Happy are they who never saw me and yet have
found faith.

WHEN the disciples saw Jesus standing among them, Luke tells us, they were startled and terrified, as if they had seen a ghost. Jesus asked them: 'Why are you perturbed? Why do questions arise in your mind? Look at my hands and feet. It is I myself.' He invited them not only to see, but to touch. And lest that should not have been evidence enough of his tangible presence, he asked them for something to eat, took the fish they offered him, and ate it in the sight of them all. They then believed.

John's account differs in that Thomas is not only absent from this appearance, but also entirely sceptical about it when the disciples tell him. 'Unless I see for myself,' he announces, 'I will not believe.' Each disciple who experienced the risen Lord would surely have riveted his eyes on Jesus' hands and feet. The last time they had seen him he was nailed by hands and feet to a wooden cross. They would scarcely have been able to take their eyes away.

A week later, Jesus came as before. This time his invitation was to Thomas alone. 'Reach your finger here: see my hands; reach your hand here and put it in my side; be unbelieving no longer, but believe.' Thomas's scepticism was sublimely humbled. 'My Lord and my God!' he exclaimed.

That the disciples were eye-witnesses of the risen Lord was of the utmost importance to the solidarity and later development of the community of the faithful in Jerusalem. It was what gave them authority; it established their credentials; 'I was there! I touched!' Each disciple needed that credibility. This Station of the Resurrection reflects the faith struggle they all had with a new experience. The same struggle was reflected too in the witness of the New Testament Church. As we look round our churches today, the most important question to ask is related to the faith credentials of those who are there. The New Testament Resurrection community did not find it easy to convince others; what made it easier for them and more difficult for us was this personal witness to our Lord's Resurrection. This life of witness offered as much as ours, but their success was marked by the influence of their Lord's wounds, seen in his risen body.

Thomas the doubter stands for all time as the model of the would-be believer. There have always been many like him through the ages; there are more today than in any previous time. The scientific world we inhabit is a world that works dependently on proof, a world where even the most unlikely wonder, if it is the work of man, is made explicable. But we cannot evaluate faith as we can, say, the capture of the electron. Faith is of a different world. Nor can we take to the would-be believer what we have never seen ourselves. That is why Christians today need such credibility in many areas of challenge. If we were to deny the resurrection of Jesus and all that it means for humanity, we might as well count ourselves as did Judas, a complete traitor and failure. We must have credibility in every area of our witness. Thomas had that credibility and we too must show the world that, having our authority from Christ himself, the powers of evil must fail. Thomas knew this; that is why his encounter with the Lord was so vital. If Christ himself is pleased to choose us, it will be through us that he enters the would-be believer's slow heart; through us that he speaks, as to Thomas, the ever-new words: 'Be unbelieving no longer, but believe.' Thomas doubted at first, but his credentials were secured as Christ chose. He became, so tradition tells us, the apostle to India, a mission that surely required in him a faith of the magnitude of a mountain.

Devotions

Prayer
Lord Jesus Christ,
  who came to your disciple Thomas
  in proof of your victory over death:
  help us to realise that we too
  were at your crucifixion in sin
  and rebellion against you,
  but that, with penitent hearts,
  we may reach forward in faith
  to touch the wounds of
  your sacrifice.
  Be with us as we follow in the faith,
  so close a presence
  that your voice above the noise
  of the world shall alone be our
  teacher and our guide.
  Keep us faithful; make us
  obedient to your will;
  that we shall say in the words of
  our inheritance:
  'My Lord and my God!'   *Amen*

Silence

Meditation

Let us try to picture
  – Thomas in his rebellious mood, the odd man out, who could

44

not believe except he had solid evidence, and imagine his
state of mind in the course of what may have been a week of
lonely brooding. Was he by nature a stubborn man,
determined not to believe what his friends told him was true?
or a jealous man, that he had missed their moments of
marvel and joy? or was he, perhaps, a man secretly yearning,
in an agony of hope?
Let us thank God for Thomas
– that, in the instant his caution was overcome, his declar-
ation of his Lord and his God was complete. Let us picture
him stretching forth and, keeping that picture in mind, ourselves stretch out our faith. Christ comes in his risen power to
open whatever human heart is closed against him and the joy
is greater when his welcome within is by faith alone. Having
stretched out in faith towards him, let us ask for the strength
he will give us to stretch out farther in our apostolic mission
to the world.

Hymn

1 We walk by faith, and not by sight;
   No gracious words we hear
   From him who spoke as none e'er spoke;
   But we believe him near.

2 We may not touch his hands and side,
   Nor follow where he trod;
   But in his promise we rejoice;
   And cry, "My Lord and God!"

3 Help then, O Lord, our unbelief;
   And may our faith abound,
   To call on you when you are near,
   And seek where you are found:

The Doubting Disciple

4　That, when our life of faith is done,
　　In realms of clearer light
　　We may behold you as you are,
　　With full and endless sight.

Henry Alford, 1810–1871, alt.

Suggested hymn tune: *ST. MAGNUS*

5. The Sea of Tiberias

The central character of this Station is
PETER

Scripture passage for study
John 21: 1–22

Passages for further study
Matthew 4: 18–22
Matthew 8: 23–27
Matthew 14: 22–33

Scripture passage for study
JOHN 21: 1–22

SOME time later, Jesus showed himself to his disciples once again, by the Sea of Tiberias; and in this way. Simon Peter and Thomas 'the Twin' were together with Nathanael of Cana-in-Galilee. The sons of Zebedee and two other disciples were also there. Simon Peter said, 'I am going out fishing.' 'We will go with you', said the others. So they started and got into the boat. But that night they caught nothing.

Morning came, and there stood Jesus on the beach, but the disciples did not know that it was Jesus. He called out to them, 'Friends, have you caught anything?' They answered 'No.' He said, 'Shoot the net to starboard, and you will make a catch.' They did so, and found they could not haul the net aboard, there were so many fish in it. Then the disciple whom Jesus loved said to Peter, 'It is the Lord!' When Simon Peter heard that, he wrapped his coat about him (for he had stripped) and plunged into the sea. The rest of them came on in the boat, towing the net full of fish; for they were not far from land, only about a hundred yards.

When they came ashore, they saw a charcoal fire there, with fish laid on it, and some bread. Jesus said, 'Bring some of your catch.' Simon Peter went aboard and dragged the net to land, full of big fish, a hundred and fifty-three of them; and yet, many as they were, the net was not torn. Jesus said, 'Come and have breakfast.' None of the disciples dared to ask 'Who are you?' They knew it was the Lord. Jesus now came up, took the bread, and gave it to them, and the fish in the same way.

This makes the third time that Jesus appeared to his disciples after his resurrection from the dead.

After breakfast, Jesus said to Simon Peter, 'Simon son of John, do you love me more than all else?' 'Yes, Lord,' he answered, 'you know that I love you.' 'Then feed my lambs', he said. A second time he asked, 'Simon son of John, do you love me?' 'Yes, Lord, you know I love you.' 'Then tend my sheep.' A third time he said, 'Simon son of John, do you love me?' Peter was hurt that he asked him a third time, 'Do you love me?' 'Lord,' he said, 'you know everything; you know I love you.' Jesus said, 'Feed my sheep.

'And further, I tell you this in very truth: when you were young you fastened your belt about you and walked where you chose; but when you are old you will stretch out your arms, and a stranger will bind you fast, and carry you where you have no wish to go.' He said this to indicate the manner of death by which Peter was to glorify God. Then he added, 'Follow me.'

Peter looked round, and saw the disciple whom Jesus loved following – the one who at supper had leaned back close to him to ask the question, 'Lord, who is it that will betray you?' When he caught sight of him, Peter asked, 'Lord, what will happen to him?' Jesus said, 'If it should be my will that he wait until I come, what is it to you? Follow me.'

Homily

JOHN 21: 17 *Peter was hurt that he asked him a third time, 'Do you love me?' 'Lord,' he said, you know every-thing; you know I love you.' Jesus said, 'Feed my sheep.'*

WE move to the sea of Tiberias, the scene of Peter's fishing industry and of much of the ministry of Jesus. The uniqueness of the appearance of Jesus here is that it includes the apostolic charge 'Feed my sheep'. It is another faith confrontation to be seen as an extension of the pastoral ministry of Jesus. Here the challenge of the Resurrection faith came principally to Peter, and as might be expected of anything to do with so earthly and exuberant a character it was even more extraordinary than others.

We can trace through the text of John the clash, or lack of total accord, between Peter and Jesus. It was no more, perhaps, than one of those clashes between two personalities which, in spite of itself, serves to reveal one to the other the qualities which in each is most attractive and lovable. When Peter first met Jesus there was a clash of a kind. In John 1: 42, we read: 'He [Andrew] brought Simon to Jesus, who looked at him and said, "You are Simon son of John. You shall be called Cephas" (that is Peter, the Rock).' There may have been something of the gently sardonic in this statement; something to do with more than Peter's sturdy size. Did Jesus see, even now, that in this man Peter, the Rock, who was outwardly a rough diamond, there was a flaw, a hidden brittleness of character? If he did, we must surmise that he nevertheless saw in him also a great potential for the building up of the Kingdom.

Peter was always protesting his loyalty. Jesus once asked the twelve disciples whether they also wanted to leave him as other of his followers had already done (John 6: 67). Peter's answer was not a straightforward yes or no, but 'Lord, to whom shall we go? Your words are eternal life, we have faith!' His nature was to blurt out forthrightly whatever came first to his mind. A simple man, a bit of a braggart perhaps, he was eager to please. When, later, Jesus was washing his disciples' feet, Peter wanted nothing to do with it. John 13: 8 describes the scene. Peter declared, 'Never at any time will you wash my feet!' 'If I do not wash your feet,' Jesus answered, 'you will no longer be my disciple.' That was enough for Peter. He begged Jesus not only to wash his feet, but the rest of him too. There was nothing of the half way about Peter; it was all or nothing. Later still (John 13: 37), Peter asked Jesus, 'Lord, why can't I follow you now? I am ready to die for you!' Again they are words typical of Peter's ever-ready mouth. How he must have regretted them! The reply of Jesus was devastating: '. . . before the cock crows you will have denied three times that you even know me.' Again, in the garden, when Jesus was arrested, Peter thought that he had the ready answer of the moment. He took out his sword. Yet even his playing the role of hero still earned him the stricture of Jesus: 'Put your sword back in its place.' John 18: 17 gives us Peter's first denial of Jesus, to a servant maid. By verse 25 he has denied him again, and by verse 27, just before the crowing of the cock, he has denied him a third time even as Jesus had told him he would.

Even if Peter's heart, in that very large physical frame, was haunted by all that had happened, his old impulsive nature was little changed. It showed itself yet again, and soon, when the risen Jesus stood waiting on the shore of the sea of Tiberias at sunrise. The disciples had been fishing all night and caught nothing. They did not recognise the stranger on the shore. Even so, his calling voice told them where to fish, and they obeyed him. The result was a catch they could scarcely draw in. 'It is the Lord!' said John. Once again, that was enough for the ardent Peter. There was no hesitation. He leapt all but naked into the water and waded ashore.

Before long, Peter was facing yet another personal testing. Jesus had an explicit question for him.

'Do you love me more than all else?'

'Yes, Lord, you know that I love you.'

'Feed my lambs.'

Jesus asked the same question again and received the same reply. Then, the reiteration of the question a third time so upset Peter that he could scarcely choke out his answer for sadness.

'Lord,' you know everything there is to know about me, so you know that I love you!'

'Feed my sheep,' said Jesus.

The instruction to Peter was what we, in our formal way today, would classify an ordination charge. 'Feed my lambs, my sheep' – be a shepherd to them; lead them through to the Kingdom. Peter had denied his Lord three times, yet even that did not put off this heart-searching question put to him now in equal number. Despite everything, Jesus had never lost faith in Peter, nor sight of his great potentiality for the utmost service. Indeed, at the very beginning, when Jesus put that other choice to Peter, to follow him, to become a disciple, a fisher of human hearts, he had seen what there was in the soul of this sturdy man and been pleased to nickname him Peter, the Rock.

Through faith, through love, Peter's sometime brittleness was to become a rock-like strength for the weak who needed it. It was to establish the church, the Body of Christ on earth, whose fundamental activity of caring would have in him a sound beginning – feeding the lambs, feeding the sheep.

As the choice was to Peter, so it is to us today. Are we for Christ? How do we choose? Do we love him more than all else? Do we put him and his Kingdom first? Peter made his best decision to follow Jesus at the beginning, his subsequent decisions caused him pain, frustration and embarrassment, but the sight of the risen Lord gave Peter the courage to fulfil the trust Jesus had in him.

Do we, in the clamour of lives that are perhaps over complicated, hear the words of his same invitation? – 'Follow me.' The choice is ours.

Devotions

Prayer
Lord Jesus,
  who saw in Peter by the lakeside
  the Rock of your church:
  you see us as we really are,
  for you can see right through us
  and nothing that we are
  or can be
  is hidden from you.
  When by word or deed
  we dishonour ourselves
  and deny that we know you,
  forgive us;
  turn our timidity to boldness,
  our weakness to strength,
  that, within the sacramental grace
  of your forgiveness
  we may be made
  fittingly a part
  of your steadfast company
  of disciples,
  and speaking your name
  with pride
  may ever serve you
  in humility and love.   *Amen*

Silence

Meditation

Let us imagine
- the shore of the Sea of Tiberias under the hills of Galilee; a region quite the opposite of the hustle and bustle of the streets of Jerusalem. Here life was centred on fishing, and so it has been throughout history. This was Peter's home country.

Let us recall
- the various encounters between Peter and Jesus, remembering that it was Peter who boldly stated that Jesus was the Christ, the Son of God (Matthew 16: 16) and it was Peter who later, as Jesus predicted, denied that he even knew him (Mark 14: 71).

Let us remember with thanks
- that the purpose of Jesus for Peter was worked out over some three years, and that Peter, perhaps because of his impulsive nature, but also because of his potential, was subjected even more than the others to a direct challenge to faith. Peter tried, so to speak, to get off the hook after Jesus was arrested. In the end, in the stillness of the lakeside, he was held fast by his faith and might then have repeated his earlier rash words with the ring of truth: 'Lord, I am ready to die for you!' Jesus had prepared him to be firm of purpose, as all his disciples are called to be: to establish his Apostolic church. Peter was indeed to die for his faith in Jesus and his love for him; as we believe, in Rome, during the reign of the despot Nero.

Hymn

1 Shepherd of souls, refresh and bless
   Your chosen pilgrim flock
   With manna in the wilderness,
   With water from the rock.

The Sea of Tiberias

2 We would not live by bread alone,
   But by your word of grace,
   In strength of which we travel on
   To our abiding place.

3 Be known to us in breaking bread,
   But do not then depart;
   Savior, abide with us, and spread
   Your table in our heart.

4 Lord, sup with us in love divine;
   Your Body and your Blood,
   That living bread, that heavenly wine,
   Be our immortal food.

James Montgomery, 1771–1854, alt.

Suggested hymn tune: *ST. AGNES*

6. The Damascus Road

The central character of this Station is
SAUL OF TARSUS

Scripture passage for study
Acts 9: 1–9

Passages for further study
Acts 8: 1–3
1 Corinthians 15: 1–11

Scripture passage for study
ACTS 9: 1–9

MEANWHILE Saul was still breathing murderous threats against the disciples of the Lord. He went to the High Priest and applied for letters to the synagogues at Damascus authorizing him to arrest anyone he found, men or women, who followed the new way, and bring them to Jerusalem. While he was still on the road and nearing Damascus, suddenly a light flashed from the sky all around him. He fell to the ground and heard a voice saying, 'Saul, Saul, why do you persecute me?' 'Tell me, Lord,' he said, 'who you are.' The voice answered, 'I am Jesus, whom you are persecuting. But get up and go into the city, and you will be told what you have to do.' Meanwhile the men who were travelling with him stood speechless; they heard the voice but could see no one. Saul got up from the ground, but when he opened his eyes he could not see; so they led him by the hand and brought him into Damascus. He was blind for three days, and took no food or drink.

Homily

ACTS 9: 3–5 *While he was still on the road and nearing Damascus, suddenly a light flashed from the sky all around him. He fell to the ground and heard a voice saying, 'Saul, Saul, why do you persecute me?' 'Tell me, Lord,' he said, 'who you are.' The voice answered, 'I am Jesus, whom you are persecuting. . . .'*

PAUL does not appear in any of the four gospels, but next to Jesus he is perhaps the most important character in the New Testament. If we count the Acts of the Apostles as part two of Luke's gospel, then it helps to redress the balance of evidence about Paul's claim to have been a resurrection witness. Saul, the persecutor of the followers of the new way, needed the Damascus road experience to authenticate his apostleship and to give him an authority equal to that of the disciples.

Saul was a man different from the others both in character and background. When the disciples had been walking with Jesus in the Galilean hills, Saul was learning Jewish theology from Gamelial the erudite Hebrew theologian. He was a university educated Jew of Tarsus in the south of Asia Minor; he could claim Roman citizenship; he was well able to relate his thinking to the wider ancient world; he had an understanding of both Roman law and Greek philosophy.

He is introduced at the beginning of chapter 8 in the Acts of the Apostles as one who was approving of the murder of Stephen. Soon afterwards he is seen as a zealous persecutor of the infant church, harrying men and women in their own homes with all the fervour of a Gestapo officer and having them committed to prison. Than Saul, the skilful and tireless enemy, there could not have been a more important convert to the new way.

His resurrection experience was different from all the others. It is placed in time about two years after the death of Jesus. All the disciples had seen Jesus after his resurrection in a form they could even touch. Saul had never known Jesus in the flesh; Jesus was but a name. So for him the presence of Jesus was in a brilliant light which blinded him on the very road he had himself chosen in the belief that it would lead to the routing out of still more of the followers of the so-called Way of the Lord. He was led away, still blinded, on the first dazed steps of his destiny, to receive a different sight, to await his marching orders, and to become in due time Paul the principal evangelist to the Mediterranean world.

Paul's own record of the resurrection, given in his first letter to the Corinthians (15: 4ff.) presents a difficulty of interpretation, for his citings of the appearances of the risen Jesus are not in strict accordance with others elsewhere, but in saying that 'in the end he appeared even to me, though this birth of mine was monstrous' he is making the point that he claims for himself a legitimate and extraordinarily personal place in an extensive succession of appearances by Jesus. He is claiming no less than that Jesus appeared specifically to him. It is his proclamation of the resurrection appearances, including the one to himself, that is more important to us than any assemblage of chronological detail.

The difference between the Gospel appearances and the one Paul claims helps us to understand something of the minds of the two groups. The disciples, who had been so close to Jesus as to be able not only to see, but to touch, had experienced a farewell. They knew what they were to expect. Paul's experience was quite the opposite. When Jesus called him by name on the Damascus road he heard the voice of one to whom he had been an arch-enemy. A passion for the pursuit and extermination of the followers of Jesus had been his preoccupation.

The King James' version of the Corinthians text includes the phrase 'as of one born out of due time'. This is a choice and apt translation for two reasons: one because Paul explains how the forming of his religious faith in the womb of orthodox Jewish theology had stifled his spiritual birth; the other because his momentous personal experience of Christ's resurrection was not contemporary with that of the others who had seen him. Yet its coming later in time in no way diminished its validity. It was as authentic. Indeed, Paul's spiritual bringing to birth on the Damascus road was, in his own words, the greater miracle. 'In the end he appeared even to me' were exactly the authoritative words the growing young church needed to hear to encourage it and to confirm and strengthen its faith.

As descendants of those early followers of the way of the Lord we celebrate this Station of the Resurrection as an event of signal wonder: that the risen Christ chose to make himself known to his persecutor, and so change him, as in a flash of light, that he became by the magnitude and number of his far-reaching achievements the greatest of all the faithful apostles who were martyred for their Lord's sake.

Devotions

Prayer
Jesus our Risen Lord,
   Light of the World,
   whose power stands unconquerably greater
   than the powers of any evil worked against you:
   we thank you for the miracle of your coming
   to Saul of Tarsus, that in the brilliance of
   your blinding presence he should lose his sight
   and gain a vision,
   that he should be your enemy no more,
   that he should die to sin and rise again in
   newness of life,
   and that through him, your gifted apostle Paul,
   enlightenment and understanding of your
   everlasting goodness and mercy
   should pour into the hearts of your people everywhere.
   Open our minds to the truths he writes
   and our hearts to welcome them,
   that hearing your voice through him your servant
   we may listen, and learning your will for us
   may in strengthened faith go forth to obey it.   *Amen*

Silence

Meditation

Let us ask ourselves
   – whether sometimes we have at least a bit of the early Saul of

Tarsus in us. We may actually hinder the work of God because we are wilfully blind to it, or we may do so because we are too bigoted, self-interested, intolerant, or simply too lazy to take the thoughtful time to examine it for what it truly is. It has always been easy to find examples of pig-headed intolerance and bigotry in the guise of the church, and self-interest and laziness are close followers.

Let us remember
– that Saul of Tarsus was a man of highly developed intellect. He was also rigidly self-righteous; a strictly practical, hidebound man not given to changes of heart or mind, and no dreamer of dreams. It is important to us to keep in mind the reason for his being on the way to Damascus. He had been entrusted by the Sanhedrin to purge that city of any of the Lord's followers who happened to be there. His conversion, despite his being brainy, was not by any intellectual wrestling; it was through the intervention of the risen Jesus himself. This was the greater miracle, perhaps the greatest and most fruitful.

Let us read his letters afresh
– to understand his theology, to learn from his teaching, to become missionaries to all – not least to our own society. In our difficulties, let us use the patience that Paul had with his fellow workers. May we learn from all that Paul can teach us, above all that we cannot escape from the presence and voice of the risen Christ.

Let us remember with thanks
– the sufferings, as recorded, that Paul bore with amazing fortitude for love of the Jesus he had once despised. It is, of course, impossible for us to see what would have been the difference to the Christian faith, to the development of the Church, and to the civilisation of the world if Paul's unlooked-for encounter with the living Jesus had never happened, but we should be wise at least to try.

Hymn

1 Let all on earth their voices raise,
Resounding heaven's joyful praise
To God who gave the apostles grace
To run on earth their glorious race.

2 Lord, at whose word they bore the light
Of gospel truth to darkest night,
To us that heavenly light impart,
Make glad our eyes and cheer our heart.

3 Lord, at whose will to them was given
To bind and loose in earth and heaven,
Our chains unbind, our sins undo,
And in our hearts your grace renew.

4 Lord, in whose might they spoke the word
Which cured disease and health restored,
To us its healing power prolong,
Support the weak, confirm the strong.

5 And when the thrones are set on high,
And judgment's awesome hour draws nigh,
Then, Lord, with them pronounce us blest,
And take us to your endless rest.

Exultet orbis gaudiis, Latin (11th century), tr. Richard Mant, 1776–1848,
alt.

Suggested hymn tune: *DUKE STREET*

7. The Ascension

The central character of this Station is
JESUS

Scripture passage for study
Acts 1: 4–12

Passages for further study
Matthew 28: 7–16
Mark 16: 7–19
Luke 24: 44–50
Ephesians 2: 2–23, 4: 7–13

Scripture passage for study
ACTS 1: 4–12

WHILE he was in their company he told them not to leave Jerusalem. 'You must wait', he said, 'for the promise made by my Father, about which you have heard me speak: John, as you know, baptized with water, but you will be baptized with the Holy Spirit, and within the next few days.'

So, when they were all together, they asked him, 'Lord, is this the time when you are to establish once again the sovereignty of Israel?' He answered, 'It is not for you to know about dates or times, which the Father has set within his own control. But you will receive power when the Holy Spirit comes upon you; and you will bear witness for me in Jerusalem, and all over Judaea and Samaria, and away to the ends of the earth.'

When he had said this, as they watched, he was lifted up, and a cloud removed him from their sight. As he was going, and as they were gazing intently into the sky, all at once there stood beside them two men in white who said, 'Men of Galilee, why stand there looking up into the sky? This Jesus, who has been taken away from you up to heaven, will come in the same way as you have seen him go.'

Homily

ACTS 1: 10   *As he was going, and as they were gazing intently into the sky, all at once there stood beside them two men in white who said, 'Men of Galilee, why stand there looking up into the sky? This Jesus, who has been taken away from you up to heaven, will come in the same way as you have seen him go.'*

THE period of forty days following the first appearance of the risen Jesus, in which he gave ample proof that he was alive, culminated now in the glory of his Ascension to his Father. The event itself was not an end in the sense of finality, nor, save in one special sense, was it a beginning; it was the continuity of the everlasting. The gospel tradition based on memory is of Jesus, departing from the earth, going where he rightly belongs in eternal co-existence with God the Father, but this was quite the opposite of an act of separation from his disciples. The closing words of Matthew's gospel imply that they were to have the continuity of his spirit as close to them for ever as when he gathered them together and taught them and shared with them his earthly life. Charles Wesley has this way of putting it:

> Him though highest heaven receives,
> Still he loves the earth he leaves;
> Though returning to his throne,
> Still he calls mankind his own.

The sense in which it was a beginning was the opening up for them of a new realm of existence, about which he gave them both his instructions and his promise. They were to wait in Jerusalem. There, within a few days, they would receive the gift of the Holy Spirit; they would be filled with power; they were to be his witnesses to the ends of the earth in the knowledge that he would be with them always to the end of time.

There is an inclination in people to see the Ascension of Jesus as something like the blast-off of a modern space-satellite. Luke's account does indeed give support to that kind of picture in the mind, for he writes that Jesus 'blessed them with uplifted hands; and in the act of blessing he parted from them' (24: 50–53, *NEB*). There are calmer pictures. Mark says: 'So after talking with them the Lord Jesus was taken up into heaven . . .' (16: 19, *NEB*) and Acts, calmer still, has it '. . . as they watched, he was lifted up, and a cloud removed him from their sight' (1: 9, *NEB*). We are blessed in that we have God's gift of freedom of imagination to form in our minds whatever picutre we choose. Yet the picture in the mind's eye matters little if anything; what is of profound importance is that we comprehend such activity of God as being surrounded by unfathomable mystery, so that it continually evokes in our hearts the utmost depth of our wonder and praise. Only if we first understand the Incarnation of Jesus as 'Our God contracted to a span,/Incomprehensibly made man' (Charles Wesley), in unsearchable love, are we able to see his Ascension to his Father as the completion of God's revelatory act which brings back the eternal in triumph to the eternal – Father, Son, and Holy Spirit, one God, world without end.

As the disciples witnessed the withdrawal of Jesus from the earth, they stood, as it were, on the edge of heaven. To stand thus, as believers down the ages have sometimes stood, is to feel the sudden and absolute closeness of God in a transfixing moment. The poet Francis Thompson, a failed doctor of medicine, a failed priest, an opium addict reduced to selling matches on the streets of London with scarcely a shirt to his back, yet claimed that he stood 'tiptoed on the edge of heaven'. This same vagrant saint's sublimely fashioned poem 'The Kingdom of God' has a verse which, as much as we may dare to suppose, stands for the disciples' innermost sense at the moment of mystery:

The Ascension

> O world invisible, we view thee,
> O world intangible, we touch thee,
> O world unknowable, we know thee,
> Inapprehensible, we clutch thee!

Only briefly did they stand in open-mouthed awe. Almost at once, even as Jesus was going from them, so Acts 1: 10 tells us, they became aware of two figures in white standing close beside them. 'Men of Galilee, why stand there looking up into the sky?' the disciples were asked. 'This Jesus, who has been taken away from you to heaven, will come in the same as you have seen him go.' Clearly, then, this was no time for a feeling of lostness or lethargy, but for obedient activity. As the disciples had been instructed to do, they returned to Jerusalem, there to wait in faith for the fulfilment of their Lord's promise and to prepare themselves for a pattern of life which, even if they did not yet comprehend it, the ages yet to come would take up from them and imprint on the uttermost corners of the world.

The Stations of the Resurrection take us from an empty tomb in the early morning to a resurrection faith; from the seven-mile walk to Emmaus to the network of roads spanning the Roman Empire; from the Galilean lake to the Mediterranean Sea; from an upper room in Jerusalem to the great houses of Rome, Athens, and Corinth; from a doubting Thomas to the debating centres of the ancient world; from the Damascus road to the appeal to the Emperor Caesar; from the Ascension hillside to whoever waits to hear the good news of Jesus Christ risen. The two themes throughout the Stations have been destiny and mission. The Gospel spread in obedience to the mission call of Jesus himself, and the early faithful and those who came later were not discouraged in the face of cruel persecutions; rather, they took strength from them and came to maturity. Legend has it that Matthew went to Arabia, Mark to Alexandria, James to Spain, the family of Lazarus to Gaul, Joseph of Arimathea to Glastonbury, Thomas to India, Jude to Syria and Persia. The book of the Acts of the Apostles abounds with courageous endeavours and with evidence of triumphant faith and fearless witness. The ages of history, taking up the good news, repeat it; the love of the Lord Jesus is declared and his Kingdom extended. We, whose lives have been nourished and enriched by the faith of multitudes, are called to go forward in our own hour of destiny. It is for us to make clear that our risen Lord is light and radiance, that his tomb is an empty hollow, and that his power let loose through the world is alone the power that stands supreme against all the powers of evil and darkness. He who upheld the saints will never fail us, for his assurance, given of old, remains; he is with his faithful people to the end of time.

Devotions

Prayer

King of Glory,
   crowned with the victor's crown:
   In the holy place of your exaltation,
   to which you ascended to reign
   one with the Father and the Holy Spirit
   throughout eternity,
   accept the thanks of our
   adoring hearts and minds,
   that you lived among us as
   our great Example,
   that you showed us our Father's love,
   and that through your gift of the Holy Spirit
   you are with us always.
   It is beyond us to thank you enough,
   that by your suffering for our sake,
   and by your defeat of death for us,
   you showed us that our destiny
   is not with this world's values
   or the concepts of our own small day,
   but with a world unseen.
   Make us into disciples
   who loyally serve your will,
   that honouring your Name on earth
   we shall be made worthy to glorify
   its greatness for ever
   in the peace and joy of
   your everlasting kingdom. *Amen*

Silence

Meditation

To be able to begin to think of the Ascension of Jesus as an event, we must see first the Child of Bethlehem and possess the faith to believe that he was indeed

> Our God contracted to a span,
> Incomprehensibly made man.

– We can read in the gospels the story of the life and teachings of Jesus.
– What has come about in the world because of the life and teachings of Jesus leading to his Cross and Resurrection we can in large part trace through recorded history.
– We are called to continue his Ministry, to act in his name against every evil. His love, by which he showed for all time the love of God the Father, is our great example; the gift of the Spirit is our strength and guide.
– Jesus was crucified, and his earthly work was finished when he died on the cross.
– He was buried, the corpse of a man, but he rose from death because death can have no power over God, for God has power over all things, the seen and the unseen, the known and the unknown, and Jesus was the manifestation of God himself, able to think, feel, and act humanly.
– The Ascension tells us of Jesus going home to God.
– Jesus ascended to heaven, for that is his rightful place, and he justified our hope to be with him in the light and peace of his presence.
– Where heaven lies is not for us to know; it has no location in finite geography and no cold searching beyond the stars will ever find it.
– Francis Thompson has heaven near by:

> Not where the wheeling systems darken,
> And our benumbed conceiving soars! –
> The drift of pinions, would we hearken,
> Beats at our own clay-shuttered doors.

- Wordsworth, in his 'Intimations of immortality', has it that 'Heaven lies around us in our infancy!'
- Jesus said: 'Whoever does not accept the Kingdom of God like a child will never enter it.'

Hymn

1 Hail the day that sees him rise Alleluia!
To his throne above the skies; Alleluia!
Christ, awhile to mortals given, Alleluia!
Reascends his native heaven. Alleluia!

2 There for him high triumph waits; Alleluia!
Lift your heads, eternal gates; Alleluia!
He has conquered death and sin; Alleluia!
Take the King of glory in. Alleluia!

3 Highest heaven its Lord receives, Alleluia!
Yet he loves the earth he leaves: Alleluia!
Though returning to his throne, Alleluia!
Still he calls the world his own. Alleluia!

4 See, he lifts his hands above. Alleluia!
See, he shows the prints of love. Alleluia!
Hark, his gracious lips bestow, Alleluia!
Blessings on his church below. Alleluia!

5 Still for us he intercedes, Alleluia!
His prevailing death he pleads, Alleluia!
Near himself prepares our place, Alleluia!
He the first fruits of our race. Alleluia!

6 There we shall with him remain, Alleluia!
Partners of his endless reign; Alleluia!
There his face unclouded see, Alleluia!
Live with him eternally. Alleluia!

Charles Wesley, 1707–1788, alt.

Suggested hymn tune: *LLANFAIR*

8. Come Lord Jesus

EPILOGUE to the earthly Ministry of Jesus

Scripture passage for study
John 14: 1–4; 15–19

PROLOGUE to the Ministry of the Church of Christ

Scripture passage for study
Acts of the Apostles 2: 1–12

EPILOGUE to the present dispensation

Scripture passage for study
Revelation 22: 12–21

Scripture passage for study
JOHN 14: 1–4; 15–19

'SET your troubled hearts at rest. Trust in God always; trust also in me. There are many dwelling-places in my Father's house; if it were not so I should have told you; for I am going there on purpose to prepare a place for you. And if I go and prepare a place for you, I shall come again and receive you to myself, so that where I am you may be also; and my way there is known to you.'

'If you love me you will obey my commands; and I will ask the Father, and he will give you another to be your Advocate, who will be with you for ever – the Spirit of truth. The world cannot receive him, because the world neither sees nor knows him; but you know him, because he dwells with you and is in you. I will not leave you bereft; I am coming back to you. In a little while the world will see me no longer, but you will see me, because I live, you too will live.'

Homily

OUR Lord is alive. He is not dead, but risen with new power for his people. These Stations of the Resurrection have enabled us to see our Lord transfer his saving work from the physical sphere of Jerusalem and Galilee to the total sphere of God's work in earth and heaven, the totality of time and space, the sphere of Eternity.

It is possible for us to see this under the headings of Epilogue – Prologue – Epilogue. The events we have been considering may be seen as the Epilogue of Jesus' earthly ministry, culminating as it did in the Cross, Resurrection and Ascension. As he contemplates in prayer how his disciples will feel and react after his death, Jesus promises them the Holy Spirit, the Paraclete, Comforter, the one he himself knows will become the strength and power of the family of his believers.

Yet there are conditions to be fulfilled. Before the Holy Spirit can come it is necessary for Jesus to leave his disciples, yet they themselves must continue to 'abide' in him as the branches of a vine remain part of the parent stem. Of course the bewildered disciples do not understand. All they see is the imminent parting, the end. They altogether fail to see the new beginning that God is preparing – they do not understand that this epilogue is also the prologue of immense possibilities.

PROLOGUE to the Ministry of the Church of Christ.

Scripture passage for study
ACTS OF THE APOSTLES 2: 1–12

WHILE the day of Pentecost was running its course they were all together in one place, when suddenly there came from the sky a noise like that of a strong driving wind, which filled the whole house where they were sitting. And there appeared to them tongues like flames of fire, dispersed among them and resting on each one. And they were all filled with the Holy Spirit and began to talk in other tongues, as the Spirit gave them power of utterance.

Now there were living in Jerusalem devout Jews drawn from every nation under heaven; and at this sound the crowd gathered, all bewildered because each one heard the apostles talking in his own language. They were amazed and in their astonishment exclaimed, 'Why, they are all Galileans, are they not, these men who are speaking? How is it then that we hear them, each of us in his own native language? Parthians, Medes, Elamites; inhabitants of Mesopotamia, of Judaea and Cappadocia, of Pontus and Asia, of Phrygia and Pamphylia, of Egypt and the districts of Libya around Cyrene; visitors from Rome, both Jews and proselytes, Cretans and Arabs, we hear them telling in our own tongues the great things God has done.' And they were all amazed and perplexed, saying to one another, 'What can this mean?'

Homily

A new beginning is heralded by Jesus. As the angel announced the coming of Jesus at the Incarnation, so he himself proclaimed an advent of the Holy Spirit who is to bring life and power.

The Holy Spirit revitalises and revolutionises the early church, the gathering of Christian disciples. A group of mainly simple Galileans are transformed into the nucleus of the Holy Catholic Church. The history of the church since that mighty prologue is a story of faith and failure, vision and blindness, holiness and sin. Is the church today any closer to a realisation of the kingdom of God than that small Jerusalem group?

But there is yet another stage in the plan of Salvation. While the Epilogue of John 14: 1–4 & 15–19 brings a continuing divine presence to the disciples, and while the feast of Pentecost, fifty days after the crucifixion of Jesus, brings the same Holy Spirit in power and dynamic imagery, so there is an Epilogue which will bring conclusion and fulfilment to the whole cosmic process. This Epilogue is foreshadowed in Revelation 22: 12–21.

EPILOGUE to the present dispensation.

Scripture passage for study
REVELATION 22: 12–21

'Yes, I am coming soon, and bringing my recompense with me, to requite everyone according to his deeds! I am the Alpha and the Omega, the first and the last, the beginning and the end.'

Happy are those who wash their robes clean! They will have the right to the tree of life and will enter by the gates of the city. Outside are dogs, sorcerers and fornicators, murderers and idolaters, and all who love and practice deceit.

'I, Jesus, have sent my angel to you with this testimony for the churches. I am the root and scion of David, the bright morning star.'

'Come!' say the Spirit and the bride.

'Come!' let each hearer reply.

Come forward, you who are thirsty; accept the water of life, a free gift to all who desire it.

For my part, I give this warning to everyone who is listening to the words of prophecy in this book: should anyone add to them, God will add to him the plagues described in this book; should anyone take away from the words in this book of prophecy, God will take away from him his share in the tree of life and the Holy City, described in this book.

He who gives testimony speaks: 'Yes, I am coming soon!'

Amen. Come Lord Jesus!

The grace of the Lord Jesus be with you all.

Homily

The early church prayed 'Maranatha' (Come Lord Jesus). This became an important element in the creeds of those first Christians and it has been echoed throughout the ages. The Spirit of the living God ensures for us the Christian conclusion to our pilgrimage. The language of Revelation is intensely spiritual. It is apocalyptic, highly figurative and prophetic. It tells of One who is the 'Alpha' and the 'Omega', the beginning and the end. For, while generations of Christians have attempted to apply these words within an historical context and failed, their aim is to encompass everything from the genesis to the fulfilment of God's will. Language is always inadequate to express all this, indeed there is no human language to do justice to Christian revelation.

It is all contained in the words of Revelation 22, vs 16, 17 & 20. Christians have always associated this end time, this time of fulfilment with Jesus' coming again as both Saviour and Judge. However we may understand this coming again, and it has had a number of different interpretations, what Christians hope is that at that time God will bring to completion, through our Lord Jesus Christ, all that he has begun to do in us. So Jesus, our blessed Lord and Saviour, reveals himself to us through the events of his passion, through the Easter events of resurrection and ascension, and in the recurring work of the Holy Spirit as
Epilogue to the Life of Jesus
Prologue to the Life of the Church
Epilogue to the Close of the Age.

Even So Come Lord Jesus.

Devotions

Prayer

I have waited for you, Lord, at every Station of your Resurrection, and you have met me there. I have seen through the eyes of Mary of Magdala, Cleopas, the eleven disciples, Thomas, Peter and Paul, through all the saints, and now I see myself with you, Jesus, Lord of all Life.

Your words of encouragement that we would not be left comfortless but would be supported by the Holy Spirit have given me such courage and strength.

I have been in the Spirit with those who gathered in the Upper Room in answer to your command. I have felt the warmed heart, the glowing fire within the soul, the flame that consumes.

In hope and trust I wait and watch and work. In the fulness of time bring to completeness all that you have begun in me and in your whole creation.

Now come Lord Jesus – in the Spirit – come and bless me now.

Amen

Silence

Come Lord Jesus

Meditation

We need to use spiritual language to convey spiritual truth. We are so used to using concrete terms, visual understanding, that the realities of our spiritual pilgrimage get lost and garbled.

We must understand that beyond the Cross, the Resurrection, the Ascension of Jesus and the presence of the Holy Spirit there is the spiritual life which knows no end and no bounds. Christ is Lord of all, now and for ever. He comes, always; his coming is continuous and there is no end to his coming. It is as continuous as are our approaches to him. So that when we say 'Come Lord Jesus', we know that he will come to be with us in the Spirit for our pilgimage, but also as the end or culmination of all things. When we say 'World without end', we mean that he is alive for evermore and that while he will lead us through death to life eternal that there is no end to that.

The relationship between Jesus and his disciples is a guarantee that he will always come, in thousands of different ways. He will come, finally, at the close of the age when all things will be made new.

He is alive and he comes.

Hymn

1   Sing with all the saints in glory,
    Sing the resurrection song!
    Death and sorrow, earth's dark story,
    To the former days belong.
    All around the clouds are breaking,
    Soon the storms of time shall cease;

In God's likeness, we awaken,
Knowing everlasting peace.

2 O what glory, far exceeding
All that eye has yet perceived!
Holiest hearts for ages pleading,
Never that full joy conceived.
God has promised, Christ prepares it,
There on high our welcome waits;
Every humble spirit shares it,
Christ has passed the eternal gates.

3 Life eternal! Heaven rejoices:
Jesus lives who once was dead;
Shout with joy, O deathless voices!
Child of God, lift up your head!
Patriarchs from distant ages,
Saints all longing for their heaven,
Prophets, psalmists, seers, and sages,
All await the glory given.

4 Life eternal! O what wonders
Crowd on faith; what joy unknown,
When, amidst earth's closing thunders,
Saints shall stand before the throne!
O to enter that bright portal,
See that glowing firmament,
Know, with you, O God immortal,
"Jesus Christ whom you have sent!"

William Josiah Irons, 1812–1883, alt.

Suggested hymn tune: *HYMN TO JOY*